KU-379-072

CONFESSIONS OF A CENTAUR

CONFESSIONS OF A CENTAUR

VICTOR PRICE

POETRY LIBRARY
SOUTHBANK CENTRE
ROYAL FESTIVAL HALL
LONDON SE1 8XX

LAGAN PRESS
BELFAST
2007

Published by
Lagan Press
1A Bryson Street
Belfast BT5 4ES
e-mail: lagan-press@e-books.org.uk
web: lagan-press.org.uk

© Victor Price, 2007

The moral right of the author has been asserted.

ISBN (10 digit): 1 904652 39 5
ISBN (13 digit): 978 1 904652 39 7
Author: Price, Victor
Title: Confessions of a Centaur
2007

Design: December
Printed by J.H. Haynes, Sparkford

in memory of my parents

Contents

Not in Order of Composition   13
Waking Up   14
Play It Again, Sam   15
Aspasia   17
Advice to W.B.Y.   18
Goethe Dead   19
Tristan   20
Opera   21
Mozart   22
His Feet Have a Mind of Their Own   23
Hocus Pocus   25
Genesis   26
Lazarus   27
Stormy Weather   28
An Illusion of Ruth   29
Endangered Species   30
Orangeman   31
Astronaut   32
Hill Farm   33
Sunday Morning   34
Time Present   35
Bird in a Cavity Wall   36
Co-ordinates   37
Harrier   40
Self-Communion   41
The Road   42
Lu Chi Reflects on the Art of Letters   43
Search   46
Cante Hondo   47
White Peacock   48
Cowpat   49
A Thought from Machado   50
Aquinas on Angels   51
A Paraphrase of Vico   52

Geist Soliloquises   53
Thinking a Dead Man   54
Ophelia Found   55
Kouros   56
Coming Up to the Temple   57
Prometheus   58
Once More, to Ithaca   59
In Argolis   60
Confessions of a Centaur   61
Not Dead Yet   70

Not in Order of Composition

What follows is a pack of cards to play
or Scrabble tiles to set a certain way.

Each has one value printed on its face,
another that's determined by its place.

About the first there's nothing more to do;
arrangement is the key to number two.

So I dispose the cards as best I may,
racking my brains to find the perfect way—

And so, you ask, isn't it all a lie?
Can there be truth without chronology?

If you are right so much the worse for me,
for juggling is the whole of poetry.

We poets palm the aces, put the cart
before the horse; in that lies all our art.

Yet you'll concede we're neither rogues nor fools:
we cheat according to the strictest rules.

We bend reality, we prune and pare,
only to heighten what's already there;

we're landscape gardeners like Brown or Kent,
improving nature but as nature meant.

—So here I stand, a barker at his booth,
telling you lies only to tell the truth.

Waking Up

A milkiness resolves out of the dark,
leaps into brilliance, switches floodlights on;
into the sudden clear luminosity
that casts no shadow subject is born,
then object. The obedient filings
of sense impression snap into pattern:
body-throb, the lukewarm pressure of sheets,
daylight maundering like watered silk
beyond the green gloom of the bedroom curtain.

The separate identity that is me,
cancelled since evening, struts in full fig now;
lopes at its heels jackal despondency—
a sense of all that's unattainable
in this preposterous world, which oddly triggers
a wave of hope born out of hopelessness.

Play It Again, Sam

Reality's gone and won't come back;
I frightened it with a wisecrack.
   Play it again, Sam.

The horn-rims grip my head like forceps;
delivery won't be easy.
My eyes are glum as goldfish bowls:
is all that swimming just to get out
or do the lenses make them look like that?
   Play it again, Sam.

My forehead's lined like sheet music;
the tune's a moody blues.
'Life is horrible but death is worse'
sings this sad-featured kosher horse.
   Play it again, Sam.

My neurons bulge with useless facts:
Tao and tyrannosaurus rex
and what Uncle Sigmund said about sex.
I'm a thousand-page footnote, but where's the text?
   Play it again, Sam.

When I'm lyrical nobody digs;
when I take a pratfall they hold their sides—
Don't laugh, for Chrissake, the bomb's falling.
Don't laugh; can't you see that matter's decaying?
   Play it again, Sam.

The stuff that zooms around in my head ...
No wonder I sweat worry beads.
Rack your brains about that and this
and you end up in analysis.
   Play it again, Sam.

15

POETRY LIBRARY

Play it again; I think too much.
Play it again; it's better that the couch.
Play it again—my only hope's
in the gaps between the notes.
Play it again, again, again.
     Play it *again*, Sam.

Aspasia
from the Greek

Hear this, Socrates: your logic-chopping
butters no parsnips.
Lyre strings, not arguments,
will bind a woman.

So take that wizened bladder
you call a soul
and blow it up with art's afflatus:
the ear is channel to the heart
and deaf
to everything but passion's wheedling.

Advice to W.B.Y.

Each day you swathed her murdered image
in Nile cotton and thread of gold,
scattering scarab seals about her
and finger rings and combs of ivory.

Then you slaughtered her serving women,
cup-bearers, harpists, eunuchs, guards,
without compunction and covered all
with a barrow worthy of a queen in Ur.

Each night her mocking spirit freed itself
and everything returned to what it was.
Now age has lamed you, is it not time
to hold your peace and let the woman live?

Goethe Dead

Sometimes this unquiet nature of ours
craves a last consolation. Sometimes
it even gets it.
Eckermann,
amanuensis *par excellence*,
could not repress his need
to see Goethe dead.
The poet-prince
lay stark naked under a sheet
with blocks of ice to keep him fresh;
thoughts seemed to swarm
under that large brow. From piety
he did not dare to cut a lock of hair.

A servant drew the white cloth aside:
what divine magnificence of limb!
The breast was broad, arched and powerful,
the arms full and softly muscular,
the feet elegant, neat of shape:
nowhere on that eighty-two year old body
was there a trace of scrawniness or flab,
nor any decay. A man of perfect beauty
lay there before him. Silently
he placed his hand on the dead man's heart
and wept.

It was the blessed interval
between crude strangulation
and the horrors of body-chemistry;
he could for a moment delude himself
that in some fashion the mortal man
had achieved the permanence of his art.

Tristan

No man knows love who does not also know
Love is unknowable. I stood
at the supreme crisis of my life.
The bird that flutters with a broken wing
inside my ribcage was at panic pitch.
I flushed and paled by turns; my breath came thick.
A vein throbbed in my temple; blood
pumped through my system, scalding hot.

What then?

Was there some sleight of hand, a change
of philtres, as they say? I only know
I drank. Time shrivelled or dilated
enormously; the fumes made my head whirl.
And then your arms were round me and your hair,
curtaining my face, so blotted out the self
I neither knew nor cared which cup it was.

Opera

This art form has been my downfall.
The supercharged pleading
of all these Rodolfos and Manricos
has spoiled me for punier mixtures:
I only run on high octane.

The green dial swallows noiselessly:
three o'clock, the disconsolate hour.
Insomnia has lacklustre eyes
that squinny through a milk-and-water haze:
even the life-enhancing moments—
promotion, that first sight of Epidaurus—
seem second-hand, something I read about.
They never actually happened to me.

Only when I ground on rock bottom
do things acquire an outline. I descry
a genuine peak or two resolving
out of the mist, and that
shakes me with an equivocal tempest:
am I in mourning for fifty years
lived out in reported speech
or jubilant at having once or twice
touched hands with Rhadames and Aïda?

Mozart

Diagnostician of our human state,
you've put a healing finger on
an illness I've been harbouring half my life:
homesickness for the kind of world
that glimmers in the blanks between your notes.

Come then; give me your physic. Only you
can lay my fever, till it's laid for good.

His Feet Have a Mind of their Own
In memory of George Best

This man sits at the wheel of his body,
a Grand Prix racer with the motor idling.
Framed by the stand, on the game's horizon,
the leather swings, remote, icy.
He waits,
claws sheathed, a lazy killer.
The crowd's thunder
is muffled now to gruffness, a banked fire.
Suddenly
without visible reason
he darts forward, changing through the gears,
an accelerating missile careering nowhere.

The punted leather with a musical squeal
flies to his instep, his boot catches and kills it.
With little imperious taps,
hungrily, unhurried, he drives it
through fanwise converging defenders
and improvised tripwires of legs,
and his feet have a mind of their own.

Gossamer spider spinning your own tightrope,
gravity's juggler, we
are the battered acre of turf
your boot-studs knead to their individual pattern.
And your feet have a mind of their own.

Sudden the cobra strike, the instep stabbing.
The ball hurtles, a flying smear
slicing the afternoon. The air
opens on either side like swathes of wheat.
A roar salutes

the bulge in the net, the curt whistle.
A pointing finger
remakes the universe, reaching
backward through death and birth
to new creation at the centre spot.

And he
slumps,
lost to the world, the trip over.
A whiff of grave-clothes
clings to his muddied jersey.

But now,
even now,
in the grey-faced moment of death,
the demon below his knees
flickers in casual movement,
thrilling,
warning.

For his feet have a mind of their own.

Hocus Pocus

An old wind-beaten ruin, crazy
with time's dilapidation, cockpit
for all contraries, all contrarieties
inferred in the clasped helix—it is
the house we live in and sour heritage.

Great conjuror, great mediator, swing
your star-bedizened cloak, intone
the music without notes which binds and loosens.
Only your sublime hocus-pocus
can stand the building bricks on end again,
composing us into a peace that mocks
Time's crackling bonfire for its own duration.

POETRY LIBRARY

Genesis

The fractious cauldron in the loins,
denied its outlet, overflows;
the prisoned seed turns on itself
and strikes incestuous root and grows.

Firmly implanted in the flesh
the seed bears blossom in the mind;
the turbulent fluid, welling up,
has its increase, but not in kind.

There is no harvest but from soil
made fertile by the blind-head worm;
art and artificer alike
are fathered by the probing sperm.

Lazarus

I became the turning of the year:
the sap not dead but balled against the cold,
the blades of marram not Venetian glass
to shiver at a touch but dusted
with rime and trembling inwardly.
I heard
a sequence of brass chords over the water
some distance off, and felt
almost as heat through my glued eyelids
a point of solstice-shrivelled light
that germed to a slow dawn.

The slack tide stirred in its channel,
its mile-wide meniscus straining
to a curve more tension than movement,
wavelength not wave (a fly could walk on it);
then the sea fleeced into a froth of ripples
that fingered up the shore.

There was suddenly a great roaring.
The draw of waters reared to thunderheads;
and, mangling flesh in their old fashion,
the claws of being took me up again.

Stormy Weather

A bulging back-lit canvas of a sky:
a Whistler sketch in monotones of grey.

And then a crooked stick of lightning falls
and holes the spinnaker above St Paul's;

the separate greynesses begin to run
and a whole waterworks comes sluicing down.

We columns of commuters under brollies
pick up our heels in most uncivil hurry

and men who couldn't sprint to save their lives
skip goat-like to avoid the travelling waves

of spray that fan out from advancing fleets
of hulled-down buses in the pelting streets.

I shuffle through a gravelly slush of hail,
my trousers sodden as a sea-drenched sail,

chilled to the bone by this discourteous storm:
can *nothing* switch my heating system on?

An Illusion of Ruth

On a day
when raindrops starred the sodden grass
a stiff-legged ancient
walked his paternal acre.
Wet feet and no galoshes:
delirium rose
from his distempered ankles
and settled in two pink spots on his cheeks.
A pint of pus
carried him off, deprived us
of half a hundred poems
or maybe a *pensée* fit
to split the lintel of the Bank of England.

On a year
when the rain gauge registered
heavy precipitations, another hail
fell on the city—snub
bullets, iron bolts,
a ton more or less of rusty fragments
with curious cutting edges.
A score of unimportant persons
whose name no one remembers
turned graveyard fodder.

                    No doubt
your hand was there, stepmother
necessity. No doubt
the grand achievers and those
whose lives are merely two dates on a tombstone
must taste the common death. I kiss your rod
inexorable, asking only
for an illusion of ruth
to temper your chastising stroke.

Endangered Species

Bring out the blowpipes and elephant guns,
the toothed traps and running snares,
for we must hunt the shambling yak:
with him it's never the close season.

Harry him with hounds' baying
and beaters walking in a row;
flush him from coverts, block his bolt-holes,
drive him into the light of day.

And when he stands there mildly blinking,
his shaggy pelt twitching reproach,
rowel his flanks and wring his withers,
tie his tail to the electric fence.

Soon you'll tire for the sport is middling.
Then try the subtler irritants:
rock on the hi-fi, holiday photos,
income tax and the telephone.

Just keep him moving. Fill his eardrums
with endless chatter. Hold his nose
in the dirt of other people's business—
and never, *never*, let him think.

Orangeman

The horse-collar of his sash galls him;
his brown boots are heavy as a diver's;
you could cap a bore-hole with his hard hat.
In all his accoutrements
there's nothing resembling a safety valve.

I've seem him walk, his chest a ramrod,
his knees full of starch,
behind the adenoidal scream
of pipes, the wheezy-oozy squeezebox,
the mournful whistle of the neutered flute.
Strange legions that will march
to the wail of such buccinas!

Once at the field, the demon clerics
ejaculating hot hyperbole
seem to draw off his head of steam.
Behold him then with hat cocked
and whiskers muddy from the froth of stout,
a ribald bucko whose jabbing finger
obliterates all difference
between himself and Art O'Leary.

Astronaut

This my ascension re-enacts
the stations of the swaggering intellect.

That first hard-won mobility
makes matter permeable to the eye:
mudflats appear in water, outlines
of villas in the growing corn.
I am the all-knowing moralist.

Speed abolishes self-righteousness.
Countries shrink to their own maps;
through smudgy wisps
of cirrus pattern issues clear:
the general hatches from the particular.
I mount the high horse of philosophy.

Next I am carried out of gravity's
draught into the black silk of space
where the mute runings of the void,
rushing, unmoving, fill my head
with final things: the vast
emptiness consecrates me priest.

—And then some filament breaks
between me and that solitary speck
of piebald colour in the inane; I cry
with terror, mother of poetry.

So my course ends where it began,
in the aghast nakedness of man.

Hill Farm

On this dour plot of square brown fields
clutching the contours of the slope,
year in, year out, the needy earth
has yielded crop on scanty crop
and kept starvation from a score
of nimble-footed cows and sheep,
though on the granite underneath
it lies no more than inches deep.

Such is the rood of barren land
the threadbare poet has to farm
and tend until his muscles crack.
With nothing more than his bare arm
he reaps his straggle of thin sheaves
and takes the strain of scythe and share,
and when the day comes drives his herd
of meagre cattle to the fair;

while tenants of a richer earth
whose cows grow sleek on meadow grass
ignore the humbly-lifted cap
or greet him curtly as they pass,
forgetting that although he gleans
poor sustenance for all his toil
he too performs the common task
of breaking up the stubborn soil.

Sunday Morning

Waking to a vague sense
of unclasped warmth beside him,
he slides a hand under the nightgown
where it rides up and touches
the breathing flesh, taut yet holding,
as though dusted with French chalk.
She turns out of her half-sleep
blindly to him and moves
one thigh weightily over his.

He feels himself stretch and straighten
and acquire a steel spine, while she
under the rhythmic yearning of his hand
falls gradually apart.
At penetration he is flooded
with the memory of a gym-slipped beauty
who haunted his school years;
she, struggling to awareness
through the hapless rocking in her loins,
gives herself to some desperate lost lover.

Afterwards
they lie broken—his arm under her head,
her slack knee raised—and think:
if only I could match that commitment
on its own terms. Each enters a plea
of mitigation; and in such a case
which of us could find it in his heart
to insist on the full rigour of the law?

Time Present

Our images for time
need to be updated: the minute hand's
inexorable reaping, the cold tick
that parcels out the world's
most plentiful commodity.
Now we have rather wrist computers
whose lizard tongues flick out
and gulp down sets of crabbed digits.

Either way, logic tells us,
we are dupes of linearity:
the past behind us, the future before,
the present strictly non-existent.

Yet love can find a footing
on this dimensionless point, as sea birds
will nest on impossible ledges
from which they launch themselves
on to some thermal and soar skywards,
drinking the sun and buoyed up by nothing.

POETRY LIBRARY

Bird in a Cavity Wall

Do not come into my dreams again.

For under the trellis of twigs
and feathers from your own nest
whose tamped security cupped you
the worst thing was hidden.

Skimming home one day
to my black-painted eaves,
you chose the wrong opening
and—wings in a crazed flutter—
worked your febrile way
down the abrading planes
of breeze block that turned
your beak's ductile edge
to a roach-infested place
where time's tourniquet
strangled your pulse at last.

No, do not come again.
I know what you portend:
that cramped destination
and dying fibrillation, as of wings.

Co-ordinates

The sun shone on Hiroshima. It was Easter Day.
  A plain concrete arch
  marks the point of impact:
Park of Peace they call it, without irony.

Wide open spaces and a discreet museum
  dispense a message of hope.
  Nothing survives; no keep-
sake from the apocalypse except a dome

of crumpled cement, the Chamber of Commerce:
  a foam toy wobbly on its feet.
  They have thought fit
to sweep the world clean of everything else.

But the world has crept back again, with gifts
  from every continent:
  stone plaques, monuments,
even a granite slab from Ben Nevis.

We stood beside it that Easter Day,
  taking the scene in
  under a paschal sun,
while groups of children on their half-day

frolicked around, loosely shepherded:
  uniformed moppets
  in artless pleats
and sailor collars who laughed and played

Hide-and-Seek and drifted away from teacher;
  exquisite dolls
  with solemn smiles
and liquorice-black hair and pencilled features

who quickly spotted two pink pachyderms
   with genial faces: us.
   Our fair-haired chunkiness
drew them towards us like a charm.

They crowded round us, gravely curious,
   touching us to make sure
   that we were really there,
then suddenly made up their minds to love us.

'*Doko kara?*' '*Rondon e.*' We groped for speech,
   feeling the small hands press
   against our western dress.
A little girl gave us a twist of sweets

and a square-set boy with toothbrush hair
   took from his pocket
   a coloured cigarette
card with a picture of the baseball star

Nakamura, and handed us this treasure.
   Then in my mind the old
   newsreel pictures rolled,
triggered by the simplicity of his gesture:

the heaps of fused coins, the stopped clocks,
   the cancers of the blood;
   a new-born child
whose abdomen fell apart like rotten cloth;

the shadowgraph of a calcined man,
   —leprous negative
   of what had once been life—
imprinted on a wall, the rest gone;

the museum keeper's nail turned to a claw
    that drops off every year:
    look, in the show-case there
that self-same claw, but from the time before.

Above all the gruesome lottery:
    the pattern of a dress
    burned into living flesh,
a shoulder-strap playing at destiny.

Useless to enter a Not Guilty plea
    on grounds of age, or quote
    raison d'état:
here law itself has no immunity.

Yet even as his hand pronounced sentence
    the child's innocence
    somehow extended
forgiveness that did not ask repentance.

And I stood in great need of his pardon,
    despite the confident toll
    of the Peace Bell;
for we are all branded, born and unborn,

with the enormity of a fact
    before which sense is numb
    and poetry struck dumb:
all art can do is by a ritual act

to register this small epiphany
    which a child mediated
    and plot its co-ordinates:
the place Hiroshima, the time Easter Day.

Harrier

East Quantoxhead, at the time of the Falklands war

The cold swivel of your eye disdains
buttercup-drift, the purple tabards
of morris men whose music wheezes
like mild asthma over the duck-pond.
Fingertip-flutter holds you still
in a chimney of air above the blue
of new wheat-ears measled with poppy.
It is in vain the poplar leaves
turn out their silver sides in whispered warning:
the sweep of that stony searchlight
pinpoints a scrap of fur
among the cornstalks; destruction drops.

A furlong into the sea breeze
I beclamber canted layers
of shale and sandstone the ocean's bite
has hollowed and sucked dry. A chaffinch
whose claws have been demi-semi-quavering
the green maidenhair flits for cover.
He fears no harrier but its homonym
which, wings slung with lethal parcels
and Perspex eye blinking in the sun,
stoops down the sky with screaming nozzles;
from under its steel shoulder a red streak
accelerates, scoring the sea haze. Hit water
gives a great booming clang. The machine pulls
howling and impossibly steep away.

Poet, in these times it is line of strike
that defines beauty and love's a stoic:
a soldier dying on some frozen moor,
proxy for you wool-gathering by the shore.

Self-Communion
from the French of Baudelaire

Compose yourself, my grief, and be at rest.
You claimed the night; see how it settles down.
See how dark vapours, covering up the town,
leave some men gratified, others oppressed.

While multitudes of an ignoble clay,
hounded by pleasure's whip relentlessly,
pluck the remorse of their servility,
my grief, give me your hand and come my way,

not theirs. We'll see the dead years' ghosts lean forth
from heaven in outmoded finery;
see smiling sorrow rising from the deep.

The sun beneath an arch is fast asleep.
Listen, my sweet: the night comes softly by
out of the east, a shroud across the earth.

The Road

after Machado, and in memory of Golo Mann

Traveller, the road you travel
is the steps you take, no more.
Traveller, there is no highway;
for it is walking makes a road.

Walking is what makes a highway,
and if you turn to look around
you can make out the path you followed,
which you will never take again.

Traveller, there is no highway;
only the starlight on the sea.

Lu Chi Reflects on the Art of Letters
from a prose translation of the Wen Fu

The beginning was in this fashion:
sunk in oblivion of sight and sound,
at once questing and deep in thought,
his spirit galloped to the Eight Poles,
his mind delved a thousand cubits
under the earth.

He reached this point:
a dawn within his mind brightening,
defining, lighting up objects
that jostled forward calling for attention.
He tasted words that rose in him like sap;
the classics rinsed his mouth with dew.
The sky was a calm pool; within the pool
there was a fountain; in the fountain he,
soused in the depths of it.

It happened thus:
he swam in phrases shy as darting fish;
his thinking hooked them up out of the depths.
He walked in language like a cloud
of flying birds; his arrows brought them down.
He netted periods long since forgotten,
caught assonances lost a thousand years.
Putting aside the blossoms of the day—
already overblown—he came upon
night-buds unopened yet. Within his mind
present and past lived in the same moment.
He touched the Four Seas in the blink of an eye.

And then he picked and chose,
ordered ideas, scrutinised expressions.

Some that were merely echoes stopped
their dull reverberation, others
kept up a shadowy tap-tap.
He followed ripples till he reached the source.
Sometimes obscure things took on clarity,
clear ones turned baffling. All beasts suffered
a tiger-change. Dragons and birds emerged.
He galloped forward where the ground was even,
stumbled in rocky places, but advanced.

And then he stilled the waters of his mind
to make his thinking steady. Thoughts turned words.
He forced creation to the tip of his brush.
At first he hesitated, then
stroke followed stroke from the well-wetted hairs.
His reason set up objects like a tree
and what was frolic in him made profusion
of knotted branches. He could trust his mood:
delightful things were sure to breed a smile,
sorrowful ones a sigh,
no matter with what speed the brush-tip ran.

And there was joy in this. He wrung the tax
of Being from Non-Being, answer from silence,
engrossed great spaces in a span of silk,
tapped torrents from the narrows of his heart.

His theme dilated as he added words
but as it deepened thought brought it to heel.
He put forth twigs and branches, scattered fragrance
as from a wilderness of hanging sprays.
The wind laughed as it passed, whirling up shapes;
bright clouds arose from the domain of art.

Diversity no human heart can plumb,
immeasurable measure, turn on turn
changing at the movement of a hand,
how can you yield a sure identity?
The piled-up edifice of words was proof
of skill alone; it was the thread of sense
that gave control. Meaning was workmanship.

The thing was and was not. He struggled on
through deeps and hollows and did not give in.
It veered off from the square, skulked from the circle,
but in the end he forced it into shape.

Those with exaggeration in their eye
produce exaggeration; those with minds
exact produce exactitude. Without
control of words there is no way; those only
skilled in the dialectic have free course.

Endless the interplay of stimulus
and its response; blockage and flow are one.
None can prevent their coming, none their going,
and subterranean things vanish like shadows
but bound like echoes back to life again.
Tap once the spring of nature, then
farewell disorder, farewell all unreason!
A gale of thought comes rushing from the breast;
the mouth's a source ejaculating words;
young shoots run riot and burst into bloom.

This brush and silk alone adjudicate,
making a blazon to fill up the eye,
a distant music flooding in the ear.

POETRY LIBRARY

Search
after Jules Romains

For years now it has snowed;
the sky so low, so dun,
that men of any size
are careful not to knock their heads
and bring the whole thing down.

Light comes up from the snow;
eyes are resigned to be
dazzled by earth alone.
It was less dark, less chilly too,
when God was on His throne.

Our fingers freeze. To know!
like mountain tarns
great minds are frozen up:
knowledge is not enough.

We have stripped flesh from the world
fact by fact, sun by sun;
but science's probing blade
skids against the bone.
drawn out, it has the stench
of decomposing stars.

Cante Hondo
after Machado

La noche canta desnuda ...
Night of silver, night of orange blossom,
spikenard night whose dying brazier
still fires the tawny earth, what is the song
you sing?
Through my wide window
the answer comes in dark staccato
tremolos, a wizard music, like
the grieving of a couple half asleep.
Their stifled wailing conjures up
two awesome figures: Love, a licking flame
that mints sighs like gold guineas
and spurts heavenward in a jet of stars;
and Death, long-striding, stern and skeletal,
his scythe a quarter-circle at his shoulder,
just as I dreamt him when I was a child.

On the guitar's shuddering sounding-board
there falls a brusque conclusive hand:
the impact of a coffin in the earth.

And what remains of this? Heartache;
the recollection of a voice
like yours and mine, that time will choke with dust.

White Peacock
after Tucholsky

I am a peacock. On my snow-white wings
veiled sunlight shimmers as upon a screen.
There's not a lady walking past my cage
whose eyes do not caress that silver sheen.

I know that I am beautiful, and wear
my head feathers with a coquettish air.
Mine is the whitest tail in peacockdom.
I am expensive, rare and highly strung.

My claws, alas, are really rather large
and when I fly it's pitiful to see.
Still, if you love me, I know how to please:
these people are all here because of me.

I am not clever, but not many are;
between my ears there's very little brain.
But who needs brains when he is beautiful?
I only aim to please and please again.

I mustn't ever sing. But then my screech
is quite invisible, as photos show.
To all good-looking dunderheads I teach
one lesson: keep your mouth shut; you'll win through.

Cowpat

I am that Sweeney whom the swineherd's spear
threaded from nipple to backbone.
My blood, thinned by a diet of watercress,
mingles with warm milk from the cowpat.

My ravelling mind has let slip
why I shook with sudden palsy at Moira:
was it the bloodlust of the kerns
or the psalter's subtler malediction?
Memories meld and grow muddy
like blood and milk in a hollow cowpat.

But I am certain these black clerics
whose veins swell under their collars
and the men in leather with dark-rimmed eyes
reek together like a single cowpat.

What wonder I fled to rain-drenched valleys
to flute in treetops like a crazy thrush,
accounting nothing good but birdsong
and the benison of milk drunk from a cowpat!

A Thought from Machado

Truth glides in murky waters like
a slippery fish. To come at him
you must direct the flashlight beam
of mind on to the depths he skulks in
(in which case you can see but not touch him)
or, baiting your hook with red meat,
patiently angle on the river bank
until you haul him out, gasping
and soon to die.
             Let him who knows
decide which method is to be preferred.

Aquinas on Angels

Perfect in grace but not beatitude,
compound of action and potential,
they may or may not predate the world.

The toughest nut is whether they have bodies.
If so, these are not natural but assumed
for our sake, as a hand puts on a glove;
in which case they are inspissated air
and several cannot occupy the same space.

His motion being continuous though a medium
but discontinuous in the void,
the angel's speed is mediated by strength,
not will. The light he gives
is threefold: circular, straight, oblique.

Angels direct all corporeal nature.
Like God, they contain space, are not
contained by it. Should they fuse with body
they leave its natural function to the soul,
guiding the supernatural only.

These tenets
are posited among three hundred others
by a most subtle doctor, and poets
who plot love's phantasmagoria
should not have the effrontery to laugh.

A Paraphrase of Vico

This slim organ pipe in white metal
pointing towards heaven, with wisps
of liquid oxygen clinging to its flanks,
suddenly has its paired nozzles
engorged in flame. You half expect
a diapason burst as the inferno
flares outwards, and in slow majesty
the thing elevates; for this
is the only host we know.

And then the miracles:
the pure incandescence of these pictures
flashed on our screens from beyond time—
they are the pyrotechnics
of the palpable world and liturgy
to a white-coated priesthood whose church
is the aching emptiness of space
or, at the scale's other end,
the microcosm of the breakneck atom
speeding towards planned cataclysm.

Granted
the incantations of these acolytes
have power to strike a world stone dead
or loose the knot of cancer; they're also
the last hosanna of a theology
that counts angels on a needle point:
at worst a mere behaviourism of objects,
at best an interim report
on false realities that will shear off
towards the twin abysses of Pascal.

Geist Soliloquises

Diffused about the world like gas,
I willed my own identity, drawing
with extreme slowness to a point.

You first perceived this as the advent
of the stone guest, whose feet pitted
the earth's crust like meteorites.
Tense with worship, your works became
gestures of magic, rapt implorings:
you were a ritual of waiting.

For a season our scales matched
and the fit was perfect: your shaping hand
made no odds between inward and outward.
But my accelerating dynamic
was your sentence; I contracted,
emptying your solid limbs like husks.

Now I approach my true realm
of the dimensionless subjective, by paradox
I grow heavy as collapsed matter.
The friction of my withdrawal
has consumed your landscape to ash;
soon sheer weight will carry me
through the pinhead of a black hole
to explode as gas again
in someone else's universe.

Thinking a Dead Man
in memoriam, J.P.

Do not put your trust
in the rickety projector that is memory
with its slipping gears and jump cuts,
its total lack of continuity.

No; if you wish to think a dead man
you must become a child again, and press
your thumbs against your eyes until
vision becomes a blur and, suddenly,
an inner optic clicks into focus
with an image clear-cut as a hologram ...

And so, dear ghost,
a child again, I see you
steady, whole, continuous. You swim
beside me down that sustaining stream
which no one—such is our curse
or blessing—ever enters twice.

Ophelia Found

Through the bridge's eye, under a pane of water,
she slithered downstream, flat as a poster;
a ripple ran her length like shaken rope.
The head veering me-wards, I bent over
and pulled her out. She came easy as seaweed.

Then the cold face looked up at me.
Something mutinous in the set of the lip
gainsaid the cheeks' indifference;
her eyebrows arched like a cat's back.
The fingers casually clenched on nothing.

Galvanised by God knows what panic
I pumped her arms, jerky Pygmalion
fighting to kick-start the diaphragm
or force a spasm from the spider's web
of blood vessels etched on her eyelid.

And still I battle. Will the lashes open
to show the saddest pupils in the world?
Or has her soul departed with the water,
sliding towards a black boneyard
of ocean bottom peopled with monsters?

Unknown world of paralysis and dread,
how shall I cheat you, how ransom her
from the piled fathoms of gaoler seas
and twenty gravities' suffocation
beyond the reach even of a gull's cry?

POETRY LIBRARY

Kouros

Imagined hydras squirm
under the pressure of your advanced foot.
Your set symmetry of stance
and hands clenched by your sides
speak of some victory, massive and hard-won.

We used to think you were Apollo:
that tense yet easy attitude, those thighs
bulging with superhuman strength
under the stone's limpidity, that smile
frozen archaic on the verge of myth,
seemed the precipitation of a moment
on symbol's march towards the light of day.

This was to read too much
into that monumentality of yours.
Set up on the untimely grave
of one whom your proportions humbled,
what were you but an ephebe-Galatea
smuggled into the stern house of death?

Coming Up to the Temple

The approach roads are littered with statues:
Aphrodite, a bronze quadriga
(the horses with oxydised green manes),
chryselephantine Zeus. And in the atrium
there's scarcely room to stand between the columns
what with Pentelic altars, herms,
and life-sized figures of Pallas Athene.

In such confusion we later worshippers
must either scale our offerings down
or climb to the thin air of Bassae, where
the god's approachable through a side door.

Prometheus

These days you've got to have a vulture.
You keep a rock at the bottom of the garden
and mount it when the fit takes you;
then you call up the technicolor bird.
With that plastic beak delving
inside you for best end or liver
what yowling ecstasies you can indulge!

But, friend Prometheus, a word.
Your blinking neighbour in shirt and braces,
head over fence like an incurious cow,
sees just a taxpayer in an armchair
with an old budgie mumbling his forefinger.

Once More, to Ithaca
Stirb und werde!

This time there will be no Cyclops
and no Lystragonians. We need no Cyclops.
Time, and these old timbers, will suffice.

The cracked voice of an ancient radio
gesticulates from the waterside taverna;
on the breakwater boys are mending nets.
Our chap-handed womenfolk
are in the whitewashed chapel, praying
to the salt-corrupted icon. We are ready.

The lines of fifty summers
crow's-foot our faces; these arms
are practised on the oar but will not fail
when the time comes. No sinew lasts for ever.

So let us look now for the last time
at Eagle Mountain with its cypress tufts
and this stairway leading to the shore,
where a dark girl is giving her body
to the harsh pebbles.

She too is Ithaca:
the goal that steadily recedes
as you approach it and that must be lost
before it can be found, on the far side
of the murderous, orgiastic sea.

In Argolis

Here where the sun's a tangerine puffball
that drives needles into my skin
and blinds the dry screes of Didymus
I think of Bramley apples.

Memory
dredges up like some sea creature
emerging pristine through shouldered foam
a vision of the green hummock hills
around Loughgall, their quincunx pattern
of hoary trees, reversed pyramids
of brittle-wooded twig and lichen-smear.
These the mind's self-adjusting focus
superimposes on an olive grove
whose bearded trunks clutching the slope
and half-imploring attitude—
as of old men bent to the elements—
are so like theirs.

But here's the difference.
Among the stones of this heat-battered place
the sun can sweat out of an old tree
a small fruit dense as jade
whose rock-hard kernel and packed flesh
yield a veritable oil of life.

Bramleys can't match that trick. But sometimes
the bite of acid pleases well enough;
and then I crave their tangy must
and know them for my own and cherish them.

Confessions of a Centaur

I

Anachronisms are born feet foremost:
gelatine hooves on stalks
callipered my foetus head.
Shrunken polyps of a mare's teats,
your milk put tang in me.

When first I ventured
on shaking stilts into the sun
my head drooped like a thirsting plant
until the archer god, setting one foot
upon my crupper, kedged
the thorax up like a drawn bow.
Taut now, I ran the slopes,
skirting the leaching verge
of naiad-dousing springs.
On sun-hot hills
I lassoed poppies with my tongue;
my infant fingers rifled the jaws
of iris for the pale splash in its throat.
The prickly pimpernel, whose vernal fuzz
is spiked with hexagons of thorns,
blooded me.

And once I saw
a scatter of bark flakes, chips
of woody nakedness, around
a pine stump bleeding orange resin
and heard the distant thud
of axe and echo, and knew my cousin man.

Grown big with days, I splashed
the wrinkled shore, observing
the funnelled limpets, pierced
with a tent's smoke hole; razor shells
like broken swords, and steely mussels;
dog whelks striated blue and green
and cowries folded round a gaping mouth.
I nosed green screws
of periwinkle clinging to the rocks.

II

Madness, or wisdom, came with the wild ponies.
Their females on the leopard-spotted
gulch-rowelled side of Didymus,
twisting their chestnut rumps,
inflamed me. I ran down
and sank my horse's yard
between a pair of narrow haunches.
Alas, my human arms
closed on the empty air:
no breasts to cup, no silk
of hair to fondle, only
the coarse filaments of a pony's mane.

On blowy days in broken canter
by sea sand or rock abutment
I watched the spindrift whirled
like ropes of pearls out of its element
and felt my own wound: marginal
to dry land and mutability,
man-gut, horse-gut hungering for
ambrosium and throat-bruising bran,
I fed my eyes on blown spume
while unforgiving flints
hurt my still tender hooves.

III

Each spring
a race of golden-whiskered warriors
trekked southward; following their spears
came fair-skinned blue-eyed women:
such women, staunch
as lionesses, resolute as men—
inheritresses of all landscapes, these!
Frank laughter in the light of day,
frank couplings in the dark; when visited
by need they stepped aside,
spread skirts and emptied bladders
in sight of all.

I marvelled
but feared them. One I loved.
She was half-child, half woman;
her eyes dreamed inwardly, her breasts
had just begun to pull the bodice tight.
I saw her once rocking her sister's cradle;
childish in glee yet troubled
by such a mystery, she sang
a wordless melody. The freshets
chuckled an *obbligato* to her song.
And I stood breathless, fearing it might end.

Another day I watched her
wring out her sun-blond ropes of hair.
Silence, but for cicada-whirr. And then
she turned her head, swinging the drying mane,
and saw me:
a monstrous creature, half a horse
and half a bearded man. She screamed
and freakish I, in awe
of her fierce menfolk, galloped off.

IV

Vile destiny, to be
such a botched prodigy as I,
begotten by an impassive god
in casual sport upon a mountain mare!
How much more enviable
the fate of men, in whom
the god's icy iridescence
is kindled by warm earth, and earth
in its turn leavened by a particle
of the divine buoyancy; whose flesh
is tenderer and minds
more supple from their own mortality!

Proposing to serve these, I laboured
year-long among the hills, enduring
the furnace of the sun. Up there
among the tortoises and spiny broom
I knew no company but that
of blunt-nosed satyrs, bristle-haired,
with teats around their necks and two small horns
that grew out from their foreheads. Patiently
I taught myself the properties of plants;
of cedar, hellebore and giant fennel,
henbane, mint and mandrake, thyme,
wild camomile, mallow and riganon.
I hunted these among six-petalled tufts
of windflower and untidy heads
of asphodel like limp and tangled swords.

And had my way. In time
men sought me out, for I
could lay a fever, draw the pus
from boil or abscess, cool

spear-gash and sword-dint, cure
croup and convulsions and the evil eye.

V

Once—did I dream it?—when the hills were stunned
by August heats I felt
a throb of eerie music in the air.
Listening I looked. And saw a rout of women—
drunk or in ecstasy, with dresses torn
and ivy leaves threaded through unkempt hair—
winding along the bed of a dry gulch.
A sliding panther loped at their side;
oxen laboriously drew
a cage with lynx and lion. At a bend
where the valley widened to a pebbly lea
they encamped. I saw among them
a soft sly youth with sidelong eyes
and the face of a dreamy girl;
his clustering hair was held
in a white fillet. Their whole scrutiny
was fixed on him; they were a single prayer
sighed out towards him. As I watched—
nor far, but at safe distance—I could feel
a savage expectation in the air.
He for his part stood silent, then
unslung the lyre he carried at his side.
His eyes rose underneath the lids
until the whites appeared. He plucked
one soul-shivering chord and sang—
voluptuous, anguished—such a song
as I had never heard.

POETRY LIBRARY

VI

He sang of Chaos: how the monads
fell endlessly through Void,
suspended, weightless, turning on themselves
like dandelion heads, will-less, afloat;
Mind was a frozen embryo, asleep
for lack of purchase, falling too
with a fall vertiginous but static. Then
by chance a single atom veered, collided
with neighbour after neighbour; the shock
ran outwards in irregular rings,
engulfing all. A vast deceleration
brought movement to a halt; the monads lay
in random order where they fell. The Earth
was born, an aggregate of atoms
somehow adhering, shot through with flaws
yet beautiful, a muster
of peaks and streams and glens under the Sky.
Mind stirred and woke; Desire woke with it
and Sky, for all his purity, was troubled:
he ravished Earth. From that embrace
a family of giants sprang. But they
were blemished like their mother. He penned them up.

His youngest child was Time, a cunning one;
he made a sickle for himself,
a jagged hook of flint. When Sky
again came lusting for the limbs of Earth
he took his father's organs in one hand
and with the other cut them off: thus his revenge.
The black blood flowed. From it was born
delusive Love, child of that pain.
She too carried creation's rent within her.

VII

Such was his song: unending melopoeia
such as the wind might sing
across whispering steppes, a dream
made song. The wonder of it
is with me still, the anguish of that rift
running through plant and brute and man
and the impenetrable rock itself,
a fault in matter, a pulled thread
in the world's fabric, to this day.

And yet the song did end. The melody,
simple as lullaby yet labyrinthine
as what it sang of, froze
in mid-note. The singer's body
stiffened and shook; he fell
with writhing limbs and foam-flecked mouth.
I could have helped him then, only the women
pressed forward on him, full of frustrate love,
and as he lay there swimming in the dust
one tugged his sweat-drenched tunic, then another ...

Out of their ragged circle came a cry,
whether of love or of the baleful act
that gave it birth, I did not know.
But knew what would come next. And turned away.

VIII

And yet I was consoled.
The bleak metaphysic of that song,
reducing all things to a throw of the dice,
gave them a kind of sense.
The knowledge that we breathing creatures

for all our wondrous organisation
are no more than the crazy chaplets
lunatic women tie about their heads—
feathers and twigs and daisy chains
and threads of coloured wool all strung together
as chance dictates—that knowledge
can break down barriers, for in such a world
which are the monsters, which the men?
Where all are misfits none are. Centaurs
and singers stand
on a higher rung of incongruity,
no more; height dangerous
but bountiful, for the more extreme
the bicker of the elements within
the greater the release of energy;
and this, once channelled from the self,
can heal with herb or song.

IX

Now it is evening. The sun
sends its last level rays into my cave;
tangled in the branches of that pine
its bloody disc signals the end of day.
The cauldron of its heat, I have been told,
can remake all things; atoms themselves,
bearing creation's fissure, fuse
and reassemble in that crucible.
Here at the extreme reach
of that beacon our colder world
changes more slowly. Sluggish ferment
will one day work upon this flesh of mine
and knit it up with other elements
into a thing as frangible as itself;
aeons will pass in such remaking. But

where hazard rules who will be mad enough
to say there is no other sun than ours?
Is it not possible the cosmic rift
may let in such another harbinger,
wandering from a different universe?
I, Chiron, can foresee great incandescence,
a lustral pyre and all things rapt
into a world unguessed at: bodies flaring
and earth bubbling like water in a pot.

X

But these are sunset thoughts. The grey that follows,
the toneless monochrome, is better suited
to such tatterdemalions as ourselves;
whose fate is drudgery and petty smarts
always returning, as the limping jennet
drags the quern stone around.
What are such entelechies to us?
The only wisdom we are privy to
is acquiescence; out of half a hundred
toilsome seasons I have distilled
two precepts only to pass on:
one is—to serve. The other—to endure.

Not Dead Yet

Egregious youth, who claim
first prize in the tourney of love,
who clank off after dragons
on a horse with hairy hooves,
hoping thereby to win
a fluttering recompense
from an inaccessible eye—
you lie in your milk teeth.

I grant the athletic feats,
having no interest in brawn;
but may not a paunchy poet
through broken-winded couch
an immaterial lance,
be fiery, tender, true,
as well as some chesty pup
whose brains are in his fist?

If not I mistake myself.
Try me and see, that's all.